Introduction

Traditional Swedish weaving, also known as huck weaving or huck embroidery, became popular in the 1930s and '40s when crafters started using embroidery floss to decorate or enhance their white linens, particularly their huck towels.

This wonderful, almost lost, needlework art form is experiencing a resurgence in popularity, and one of the most popular uses for this needlework style is with making afghans using monk's cloth. Monk's cloth is easy to work with, and I've found that the more it's washed, the softer it gets, making this the perfect fabric for creating cozy afghans, throws or baby blankets. Any of the afghan designs in this book are suitable for everyone from the beginner to the more experienced stitcher.

It's good to note that while you may prefer to make afghans using these designs, they can also be used to make any number of other projects like pillows, table runners or even towels. Just use as much of the design as you want to create the look you're going for.

It was a pleasure creating these new designs, and I hope you have as much fun with them as I did. Happy weaving!

Katherine Kennedy

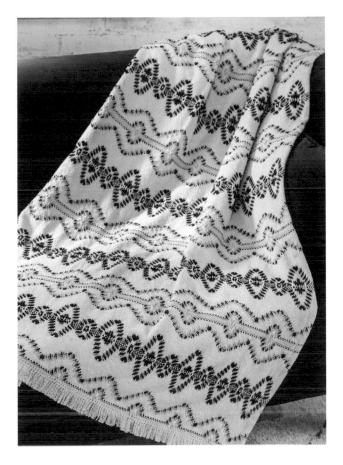

Meet the Designer

Katherine Kennedy is passionate about Swedish weaving and has been stitching for over 15 years. With her other passion being creativity, it seemed only natural for her to create her own designs, which she has been doing from the beginning. Once she discovered Swedish weaving, she wanted to share it with others, so she started teaching. It was her students who really encouraged her to look into publishing her design patterns. Just over a year after discovering Swedish weaving, her first book *Easy-Does-It Swedish Weave Towels* was published. Since then, she has developed a full line of chart packs and kits that are distributed worldwide and has designed two more books and a video. This is her third book published by Annie's.

Katherine has been inspired by some of the old pattern books from the 1930s and '40s. All of her designs are original with a contemporary flair, but she also tries to maintain a more traditional look when creating a design. She and her husband, Mark, live in Minnesota. They have six children and three grandchildren, whom they love spending time with. To see more of Katherine's patterns, visit www.AnniesCraftStore.com and the website www.swedishweavedesigns.com.

Table of Contents

General Instructions

The colorful patterns of Swedish weaving, or huck embroidery as it is also called, are created by weaving colored strands of yarn under the vertical raised threads occurring at regular intervals on the fabric surface, similar to a darning stitch. In Swedish weaving and huck embroidery, these vertical threads are called "floats."

Photo 1

Fabrics

Monk's cloth (Photo 2) is a heavy fabric originally made from worsted wool and used for monk's habits. Really! Linen monk's cloth is still used for monk's habits or as a base for rug hooking. But the 100 percent cotton variety is a 4 thread x 4 thread, 7-count basket weave available in many colors. It is used in Swedish weaving for afghans.

Photo 2

It is important to prewash monk's cloth because it can shrink up to 15 percent. Always zigzag stitch, serge or bind the cut edges prior to washing to prevent fraying. This fabric will soften with each wash, which is another feature that makes it great for afghans.

Yarn

Worsted- and sport-weight **yarns** work well on monk's cloth, because they match the weight of the fabric. Fingering-weight yarns are usually too fine and get lost in the heavier monk's cloth threads. Be sure to choose a yarn that will not shrink. Design density determines how much yarn is needed on the larger monk's cloth projects. Most designs will use one to two skeins of yarn to make a lap blanket.

Needles

A **bodkin** (Photo 3) is a flat needle, either with or without a bent tip, with a large eye used exclusively for stitching on monk's cloth. The eye is large enough to accept yarns. Another needle that works well on monk's cloth is a **Susan Bates 5-inch steel weaving needle**. It is similar in size to the size 13 tapestry needle. Because of its length, you can make quick work of a row of stitching, especially when doing a significant number of straight stitches.

A **size 13 tapestry needle**, either straight tip or bent tip, is another option. For finishing edges with the Nun stitch or other hand-finishing method, the **size 20 tapestry needle** works well.

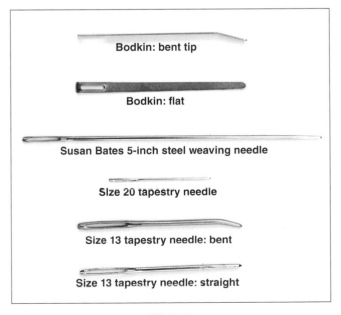

Bodkin: bent tip

Bodkin: flat

Susan Bates 5-inch steel weaving needle

Size 20 tapestry needle

Size 13 tapestry needle: bent

Size 13 tapestry needle: straight

Photo 3

General Tools

Stitchers have found a number of general tools that work well for Swedish weaving.

Position a throw pillow on your lap under your project. The pillow raises the project up several inches and holds it in place, providing a relaxing stitching platform.

Any needlecraft requires **good lighting**. Good lighting increases contrast, which will help with finding the floats on the fabric. It reduces glare, which helps to reduce eye strain and headaches and helps you work longer. A low heat bulb or lamp is more comfortable to work under for long periods of time. There are daylight bulbs you can use in your regular lamp, or there are lamps manufactured specifically for needlework, some complete with a magnifying glass!

For trimming yarn, fringe or projects to size, the best tools are a **rotary cutter and mat and a clear ruler**. Cutting mats come in a wide range of sizes. Choose a size that handles the sizes of projects you normally do.

Use **fabric marking tools** whose marks can be easily removed from your project. The best choices for marking on monk's cloth are pens that are air and water removable. Remember that the air erase pens are only visible for a short time.

Weaving Designs

You will need the following basic sewing supplies and equipment to complete the projects in this book:

- Sewing machine in good working order
- General-purpose thread in appropriate colors
- Straight pins, safety pins and pincushion
- Seam ripper
- Measuring tools
- Iron, ironing board and pressing cloths
- Scissors
- Serger (optional)

Each pattern will have a materials list that will indicate the suggested amount of monk's cloth and yarn needed to complete the project.

Individual project instructions will indicate how many lengths of yarn are needed to complete each row of a pattern. A **length of yarn** is a piece of yarn equal to one width of your fabric (Figure 1). For example, if a pattern indicates two lengths of yarn for a row, cut a piece of yarn two times the width of the fabric piece being used.

2 Lengths of Yarn

Figure 1

When measuring yarn, do not stretch it but allow it to lay across the fabric. Unless indicated otherwise, a single cut of yarn in the instructed length will be used to complete a row.

To find the center of the fabric and the starting point for all designs included in this book, fold the fabric in half lengthwise and then again widthwise. The point where they come together is the center of the fabric. Mark this spot with a fabric marking pen, a contrasting piece of yarn or a safety pin.

If necessary, carefully count floats or measure to the position to begin weaving as indicated in the individual pattern instructions.

Weave your length of yarn under the float (it's not always a center float) as indicated in the pattern and draw up the yarn until the float is at the center of the length of yarn (Figure 2).

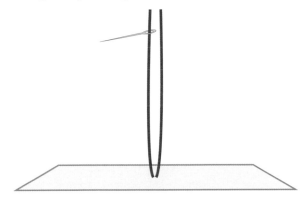

Figure 2

Begin weaving the first row in the design referring to the instructions and chart, working from the middle of the project out to the left (reverse if left-handed). When the first half of the row is completed, turn the project and the chart upside down and work the second half of the first row from the center out.

Repeat to weave the remaining rows of the design.

Secure the ends of each row either by tucking it to the back and running through 2 to 3 floats or, if fringing the sides, run the yarn all the way to the end using straight stitches on the front of the fabric.

Finish edges as desired.

Swedish Weaving Stitch Guide

The following stitches are used to create the designs in this book. Arrows on the stitch diagrams indicate the direction yarn should be woven under the floats, and numerals indicate the order of weaving. All Swedish weaving stitches are woven from right to left (unless left-handed).

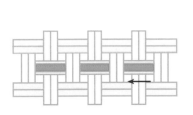

Straight Stitch   **Slant Stitch**

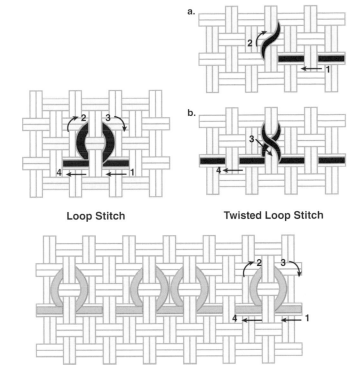

a.

b.

Loop Stitch   **Twisted Loop Stitch**

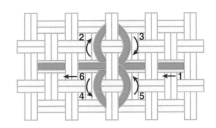

Multiple Loop Stitch

Figure 8/Double Loop Stitch

Specialty Stitches & Techniques

Sometimes a design calls for more than one length of yarn to be stitched through the same float. Figure 3 and Photo 4 show three different slant stitches being stitched through the same float.

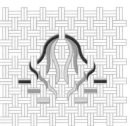

Figure 3

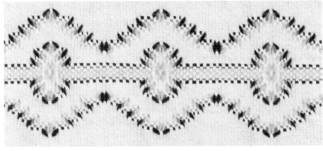

Photo 4

The **triple loop stitch** is a specialty stitch Katherine Kennedy created and is used in some of the designs for this book.

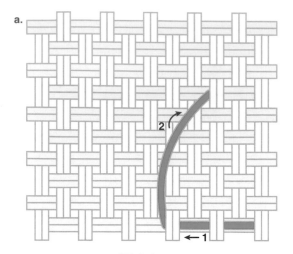

Triple Loop a

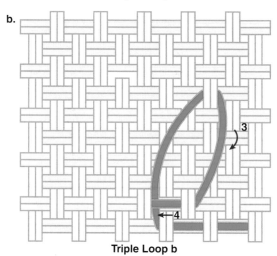

Triple Loop b

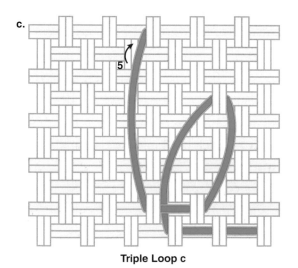

Triple Loop c

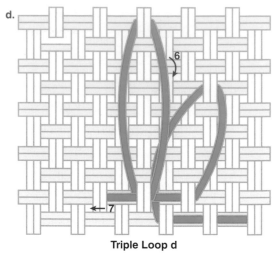

Triple Loop d

Triple Loop e

Triple Loop f

Finishing Stitches & Techniques

After all stitching is complete, trim the yarn to about ¾ inch, unless fringing. Thread ends will be tucked inside when sides are machine-stitched.

When fringing an afghan, either a machine stitch just under the last row of stitching or stitching a **Nun stitch** will keep the fabric from fraying beyond the fringe. Using matching thread to stitch the Nun stitch or long threads pulled from the edges of the project will ensure that the thread is a perfect match and will not be seen. *Note: If not using threads pulled from the fabric, the thread used for the Nun stitch should be either perle cotton #5 or something similar.*

Pull the needle and thread up from the wrong side, leaving about a 4–5-inch tail, just below the final row of the design.

Refer to Photos 5a–d to complete the Nun stitch, pulling the thread completely through to the wrong side of the fabric at each step and working from right to left.

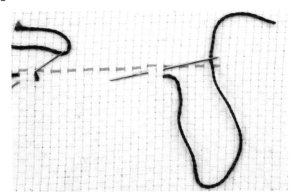

Photo 5a

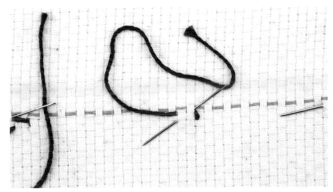

Photo 5b

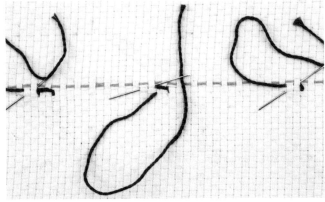

Photo 5c

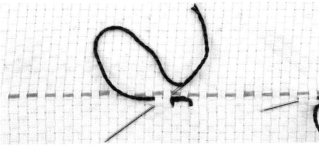

Photo 5d

When completed, the Nun stitch row will look similar to a blanket stitch (Photo 5e). Push the thread through to the wrong side.

Photo 5e

Secure both thread tails to the wrong side of the project by running them through 4 or 5 floats above the stitch line and then double back through the floats.

Cut fabric to be fringed to desired length and fringe the project by removing all horizontal threads up to the Nun stitch row as shown in Photo 5f. Note that the rule of thumb for any project that is finished with a combination of fringing and hemming is to make the fringe first. ●

Photo 5f

Leapfrog

Enjoy evenings on the porch listening to the wonderful sounds of summer wrapped in this cozy afghan.

Finished Size

42 inches wide x 70 inches long (including fringe)

Skill Level

Easy

Materials

- Monk's cloth:
  2½ yds natural
- Medium (worsted) weight acrylic yarn:
  300 yds each olive and avocado
- Susan Bates 5-inch steel weaving needle, size 13 tapestry needle or a bodkin
- Basic sewing tools and supplies

Project Note

Refer to General Instructions for fabric preparation, stitch instructions and finishing techniques.

Yarn Lengths

All Rows: 2½ lengths

Weaving the Design

1. Mark center of fabric. The red arrow on the chart indicates the center and starting point of your design.

2. Using darker shade of yarn, at the first float to the right of center, pull the needle and thread through until half of your yarn is on either side of the float. Starting with a triple loop stitch, stitch from that point to the left (reverse if left-handed), following the chart. Note that when stitching the diagonal straight stitches, you will skip over two floats, then stitch under one float, then skip over two, under one, etc. as shown on the chart (*see photo*).

3. Continue stitching design until you are about 1½ inches from the edge. Push the needle and yarn to the back and secure the yarn by running under 3–4 floats.

4. Turn the fabric and chart upside down and finish stitching the other half of Row 1.

5. For Row 2, stitch using the lighter shade of yarn. Continue stitching rows, as shown on chart, alternating yarn colors, until afghan is desired length.

6. To finish the bottom half of the afghan, turn both the afghan and the chart and complete this half just as you did the top half.

Finishing

After stitching is complete, see General Instructions for finishing techniques and finish as desired. ●

6
5
4

3
2
1

When stitching each diagonal row, stitch under 1 float to start, then skip over 2, repeating pattern until row is finished (see close-up photo of finished afghan).

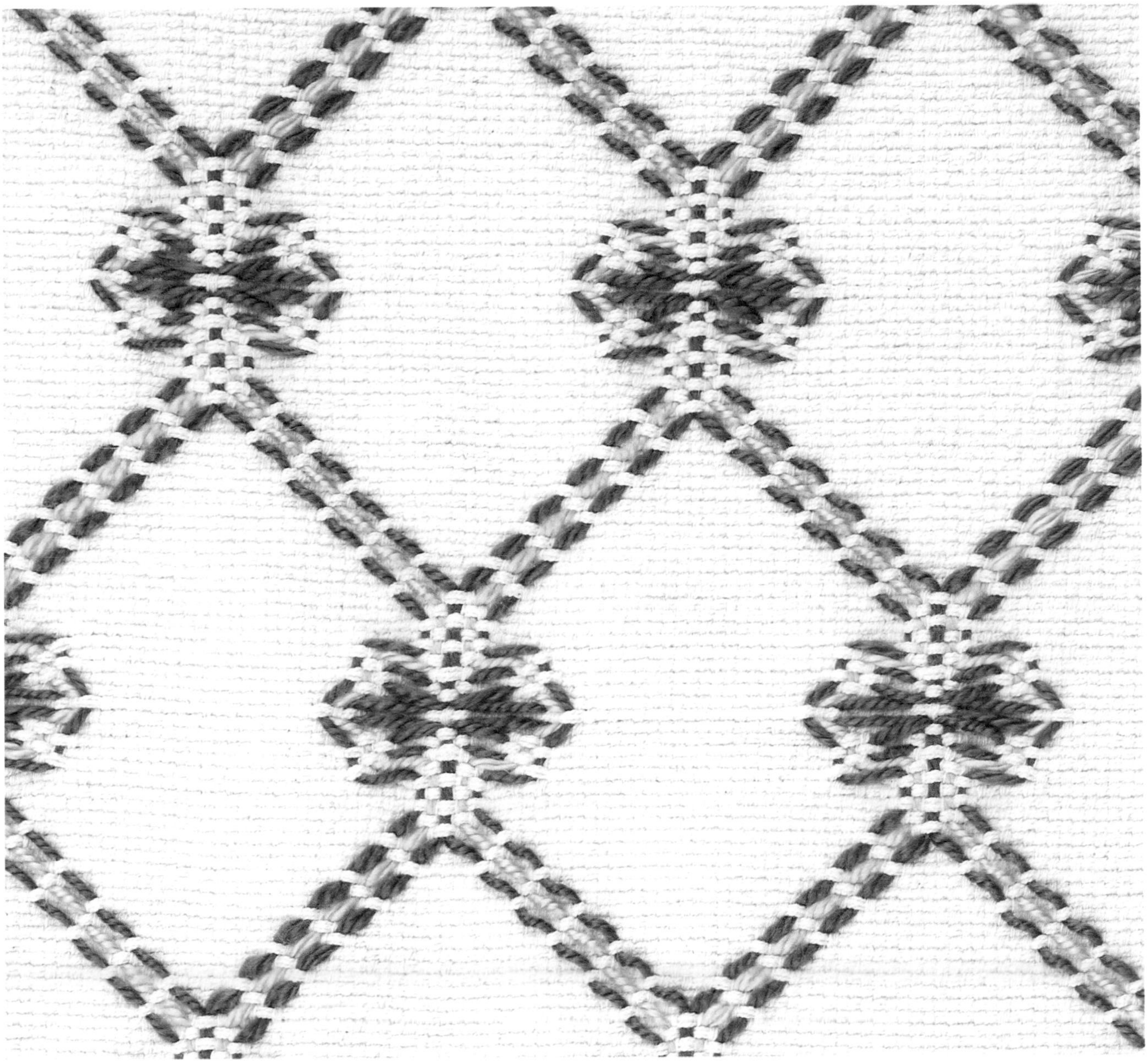

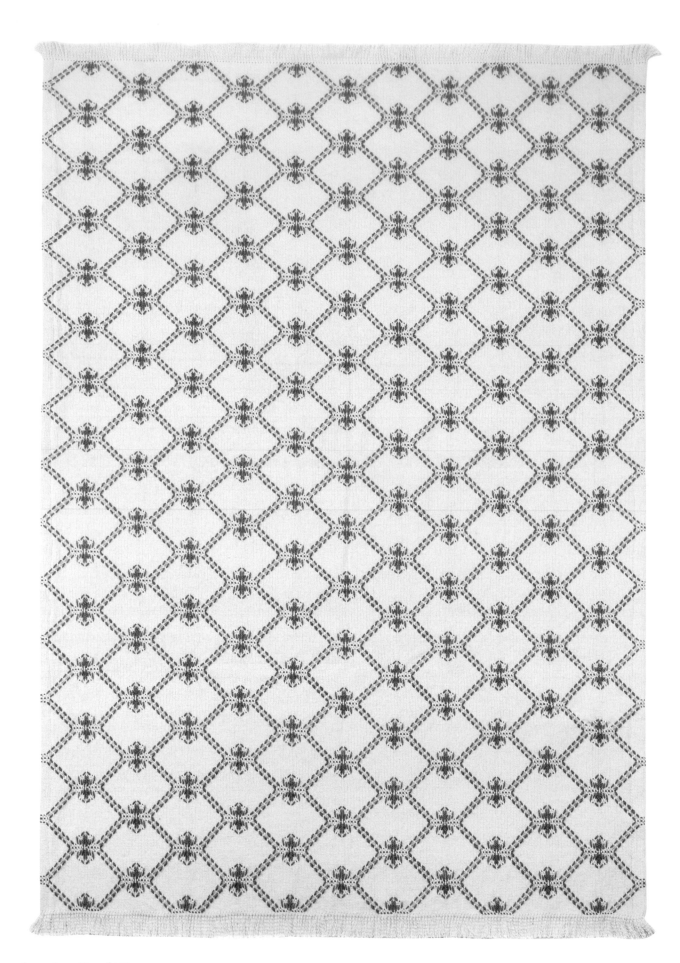

Oasis

This lovely afghan will be perfect on those cool, dry evenings.

Finished Size
47 inches wide x 67 inches long (including fringe)

Skill Level
Easy

Materials
- Monk's cloth:
  2½ yds natural
- Medium (worsted) or fine (sport) weight acrylic yarn:
  300 yds each navy, medium blue and periwinkle
- Susan Bates 5-inch steel weaving needle, size 13 tapestry needle or a bodkin
- Basic sewing tools and supplies

Project Note
Refer to General Instructions for fabric preparation, stitch instructions and finishing techniques.

Yarn Lengths
Rows 1–4: 2 lengths

Rows 5–7, 11 & 12: 2½ lengths

Rows 8–10 & 13–15: 3 lengths

Weaving the Design
1. Mark center of fabric. The red arrow on the chart indicates the center and starting point of your design.

2. At that point, pull the needle and yarn through the center float, until half of your yarn is on either side of the float. Starting with a figure-8 stitch and a 2-length piece of the lightest color of yarn, stitch from that point to the left (reverse if left-handed), following the chart. Continue stitching until you are about 1½ inches from the edge. Push the needle and yarn to the back and secure the yarn by running under 3–4 floats.

3. Turn the fabric and chart upside down and finish stitching the other half of Row 1.

4. Continue stitching up the fabric, following the chart, finishing with a section of Rows 1–4, and alternating yarn colors as shown on the chart. Note that on the last row, you will stitch a loop stitch, in place of the figure-8 stitch.

5. When turning the fabric around to complete the bottom half of the afghan, you will start with Row 2 on the chart.

Finishing
After stitching is complete, see General Instructions for finishing techniques and finish as desired. ●

15
14
13
11,12
10
9
8

7
6
5

4
3
2
1

Sierra

Whether in the mountains or your backyard, this afghan stitched in your favorite colors will be what you reach for to wrap up in as you sit by a crackling fire.

Finished Size
43 inches wide x 57 inches long (including fringe)

Skill Level
Easy

Materials
- Monk's cloth:
  2½ yds gray
- Medium (worsted) weight acrylic yarn:
  700 yds gray
- Susan Bates 5-inch steel weaving needle, size 13 tapestry needle or a bodkin
- Basic sewing tools and supplies

Project Note
Refer to General Instructions for fabric preparation, stitch instructions and finishing techniques.

Yarn Lengths
Rows 1, 5 & 6: 2½ lengths

Rows 2–4: 2 lengths

Row 7: 3 lengths

Rows 8–14: 3½ lengths

Weaving the Design
1. Mark center of fabric. The red arrow on the chart indicates the center and starting point of your design.

2. At that point, pull the needle and yarn through the center float, until half of your yarn is on either side of the float. Starting with a 2½-length piece of yarn, stitch from that point to the left (reverse if left-handed), following chart. Continue stitching until you are about 1½ inches from the edge. Push the needle and yarn to the back and secure the yarn by running under 3–4 floats.

3. Turn the fabric and chart upside down and finish stitching the other half of Row 1.

4. Continue stitching up the fabric, following the chart.

5. After completing Rows 1–14, repeat Rows 1–12. Then repeat this entire sequence to complete the stitching on the top half of your afghan.

6. When turning the fabric around to complete the bottom half of the afghan, you will start with Row 2 on the chart. Stitch sequence of rows just as you did for the top half of the afghan design.

Finishing
After stitching is complete, see General Instructions for finishing techniques and finish as desired. ●

Notes: After completing rows 1–14, turn fabric and pattern and continue stitching, starting with Row 12 and working back to Row 1. Continue stitching, creating 1 complete section that is identical to the full section just completed.

Sierra

Rows
14
13
12
11
10
9
8
7
6
5
4
3
2
1

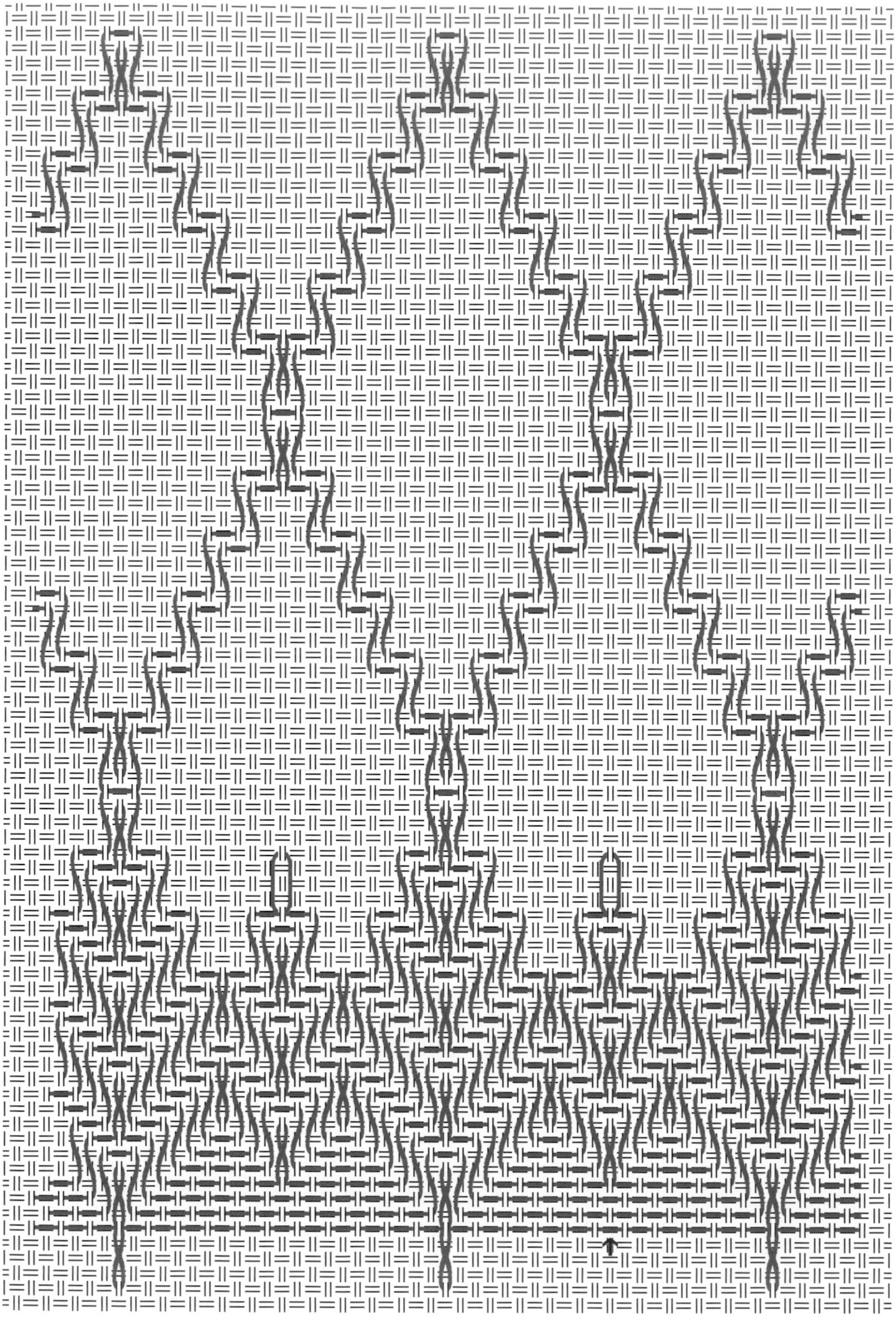

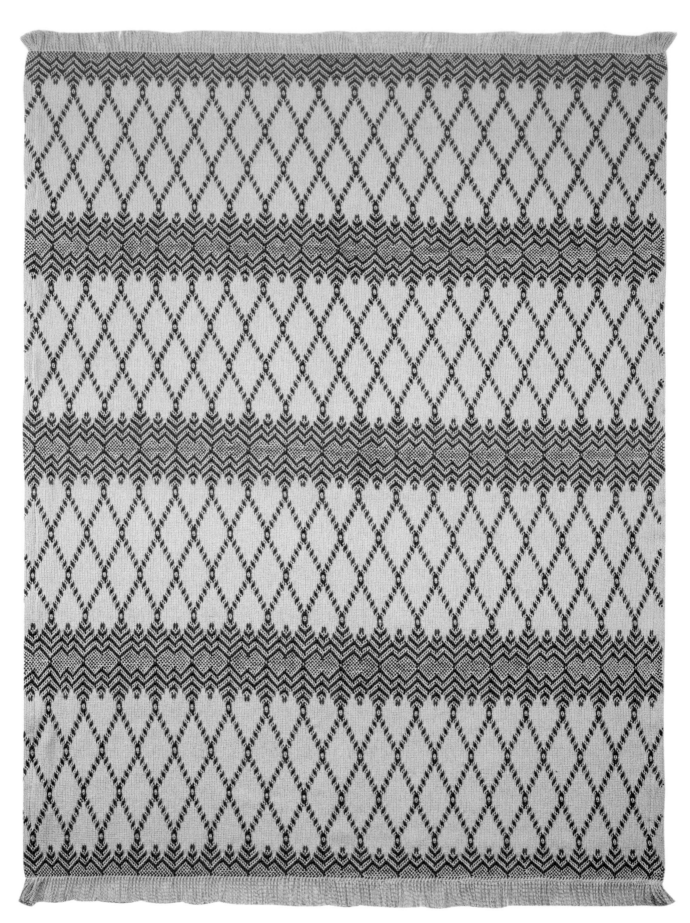

Gemstones

Any parent willl cherish this lovely afghan created especially for their new baby. It is sure to become a treasured heirloom.

Finished Size
42 inches wide x 50 inches long (including fringe)

Skill Level
Easy

Materials
- Monk's cloth:
  2 yds white
- Medium (worsted) or fine (sport) weight acrylic yarn:
  500 yds each periwinkle and medium blue
  250 yds variegated
- Susan Bates 5-inch steel weaving needle, size 13 tapestry needle or a bodkin
- Basic sewing tools and supplies

Project Note
Refer to General Instructions for fabric preparation, stitch instructions and finishing techniques.

Yarn Lengths
Rows 1, 6 & 7: 3 lengths

Rows 2–5, 8 & 9: 2½ lengths

Rows 10–15: 3½ lengths

Weaving the Design
1. Mark center of fabric. The red arrow on the chart indicates the center and starting point of your design.

2. Starting with a 3-length piece of the variegated yarn, at the first float to the right of center, pull the needle and yarn through until half of your yarn is on either side of the float. Starting with a triple loop stitch, stitch from that point to the left (reverse if left-handed), following the chart. There are 7 straight stitches between each triple loop stitch in this first row. Continue stitching until you are about 1½ inches from the edge. Push the needle and yarn to the back and secure the yarn by running under 3–4 floats.

3. Turn the fabric and chart upside down and finish stitching the other half of Row 1.

4. Stitch Row 2, using a 2½-length of the darker shade of solid yarn. Note that on Rows 2, 3, 4, 5, 8 and 9 as shown on the chart, when doing the diagonal straight stitches, you will skip over two floats, stitch under two floats and skip over two floats. For Rows 10–15, you just skip over the two center floats on the diagonal section of stitching (see photos).

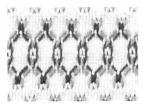

5. Continue stitching, following the chart, using the appropriate color of yarn per row as shown on the chart.

6. After finishing Row 15, turn the chart and work down the chart from Row 15 to Row 1.

7. After getting back to Row 1, turn the chart once again and stitch up to Row 11. This will be the final row of the afghan.

8. To finish the bottom half of the afghan, turn both the afghan and the chart and complete this half just as you did the top half.

Finishing
After stitching is complete, see General Instructions for finishing techniques and finish as desired. ●

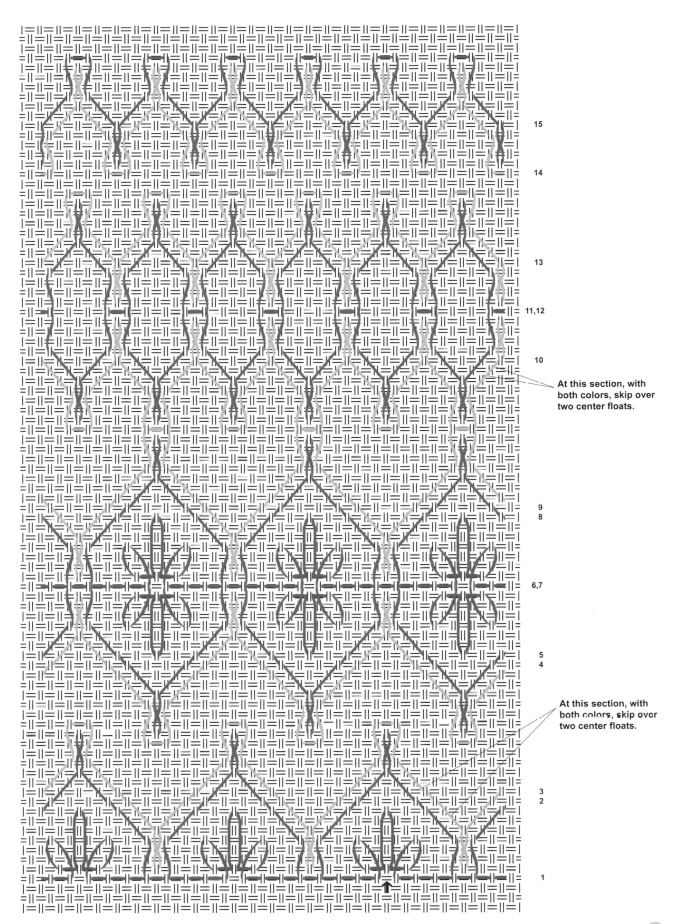

15

14

13

11,12

10

At this section, with
both colors, skip over
two center floats.

9
8

6,7

5
4

At this section, with
both colors, skip over
two center floats.

3
2

1

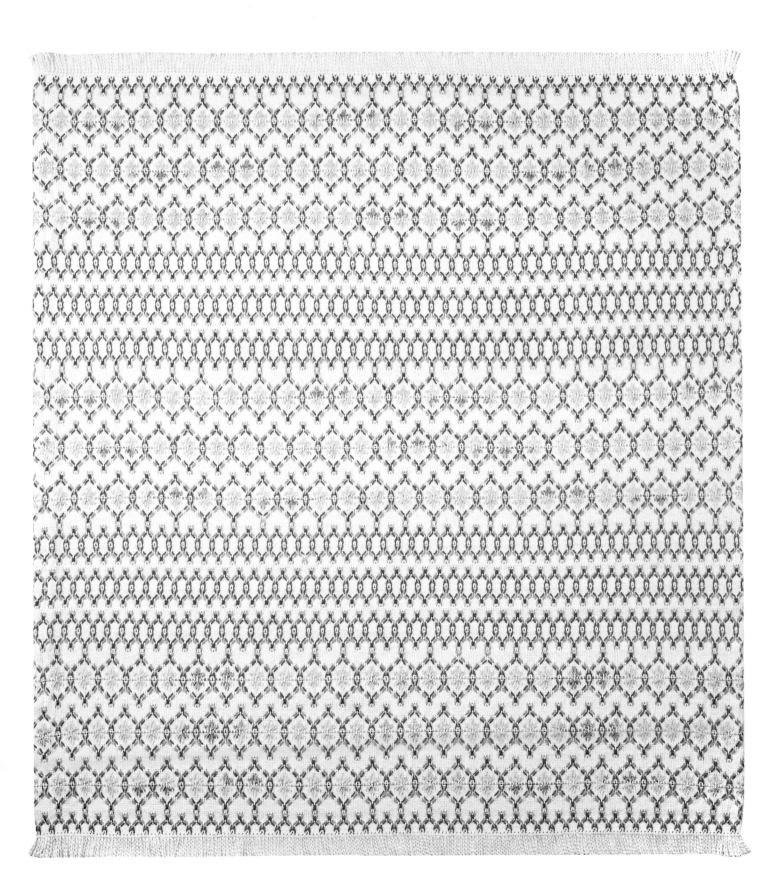

Rock Candy

This fun design, reminiscent of the treat we enjoyed as a child, can be done in any color combination to complement your decor.

Finished Size

43 inches wide x 53 inches long (including fringe)

Skill Level

Easy

Materials

- Monk's cloth:
  2½ yds vanilla bean
- Medium (worsted) weight acrylic yarn:
  252 yds each teal and matching variegated
- Susan Bates 5-inch steel weaving needle, size 13 tapestry needle or a bodkin
- Basic sewing tools and supplies

Project Note

Refer to General Instructions for fabric preparation, stitch instructions and finishing techniques.

Yarn Lengths

Rows 1 & 9: 5 lengths

Rows 2, 7 & 8: 2½ lengths

Rows 3–6: 3 lengths

Weaving the Design

1. Mark center of fabric. The red arrow on the chart indicates the center and starting point of your design.

2. Using a 5-length piece of the variegated yarn, at the first float pull the needle and yarn through until half of your yarn is on either side of the float. Starting with a twisted loop stitch, one above and one below the centerline, stitch from that point, to the left (reverse if left-handed), following the chart. Continue stitching until you are about 1½ inches from the edge. Push the needle and yarn to the back and secure the yarn by running under 3–4 floats.

3. Turn the fabric and chart upside down and finish stitching the other half of Row 1.

4. For Row 2, stitch using the teal yarn, noting that where indicated Rows 1 and 2 share floats. Continue stitching rows as shown on chart, alternating yarn colors, until afghan is desired length.

5. To finish the bottom half of the afghan, turn both the afghan and the chart and complete this half just as you did the top half.

Finishing

After stitching is complete, see General Instructions for finishing techniques and finish as desired. ●

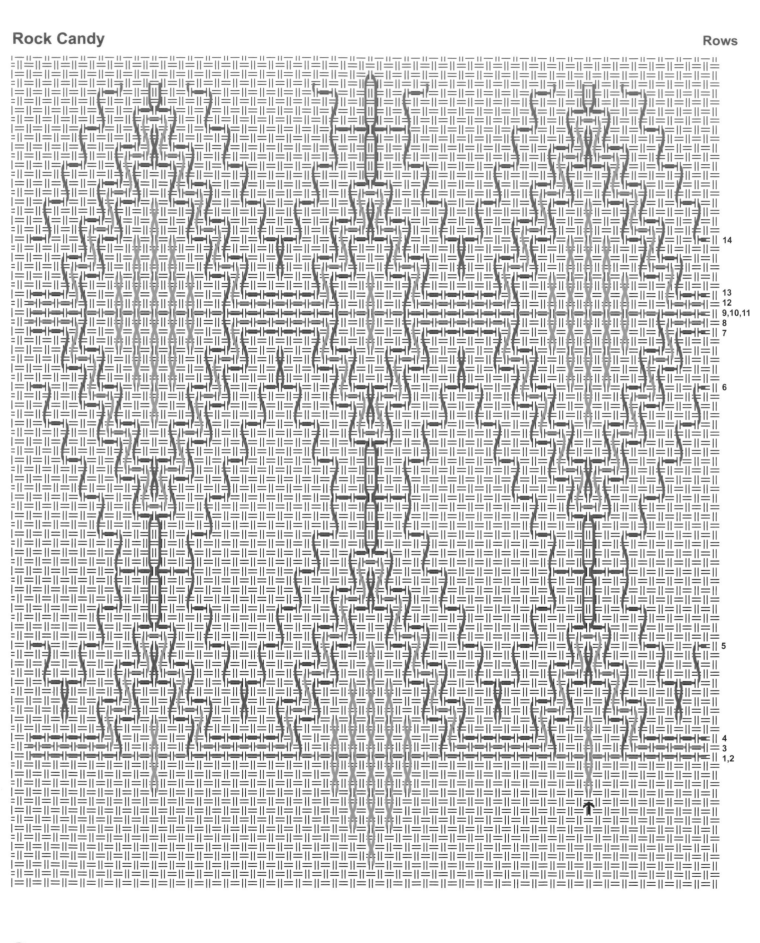

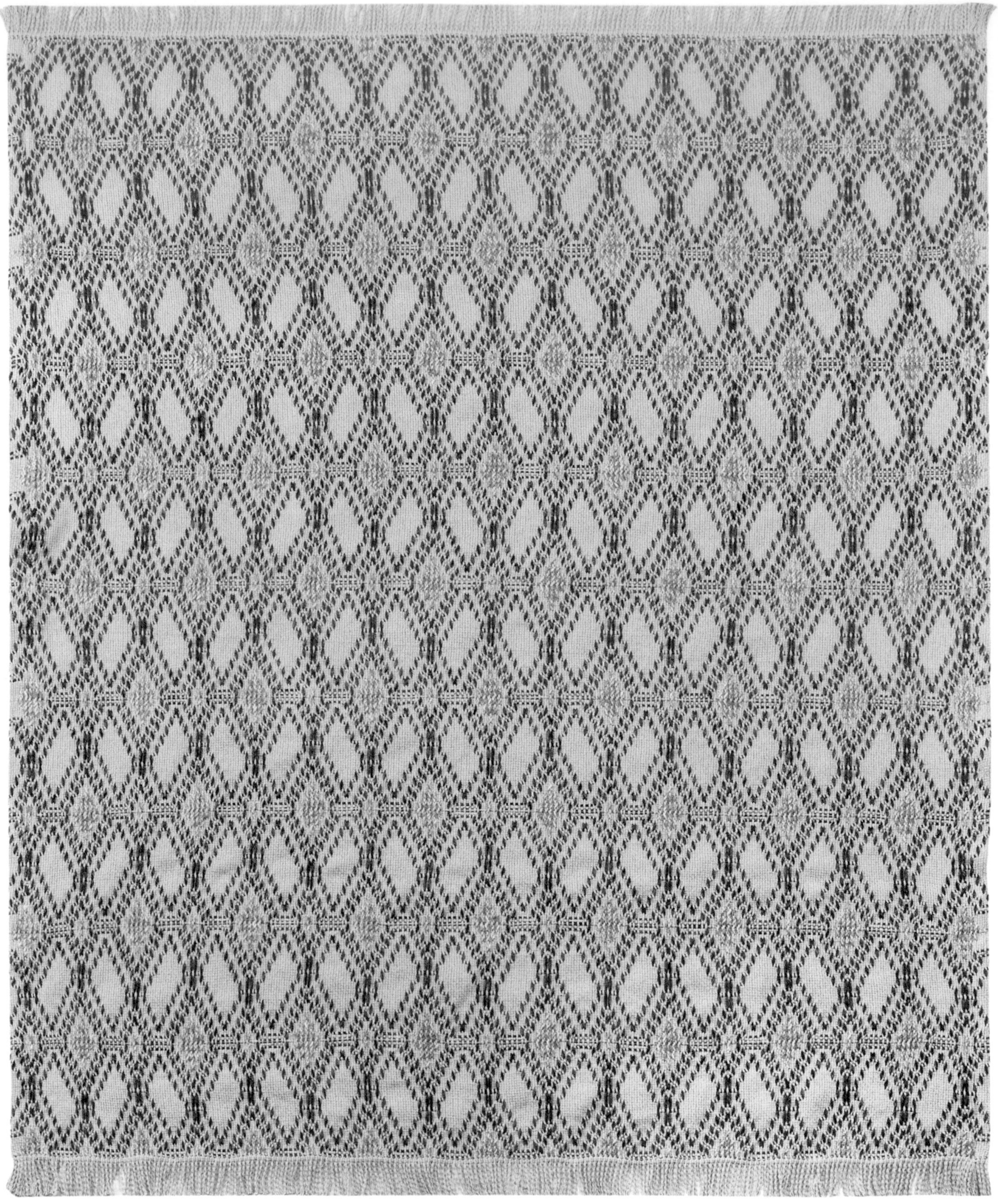

Surf

You can almost envision the waves crashing on the shore as you snuggle up in this cozy afghan, created to resemble the colors of water and sand coming together in perfect harmony.

Finished Size
44 inches wide x 68 inches long (including fringe)

Skill Level
Intermediate

Materials
- Monk's cloth:
  2½ yds natural
- Medium (worsted) weight acrylic yarn:
  256 yds turquoise
  204 yds matching variegated
- Susan Bates 5-inch steel weaving needle, size 13 tapestry needle or a bodkin
- Basic sewing tools and supplies

Project Note
Refer to General Instructions for fabric preparation, stitch instructions and finishing techniques.

Yarn Lengths
Rows 1–3: 2 lengths

Rows 4–7 & 13–18: 2½ lengths

Rows 8–12: 3 lengths

Weaving the Design

1. Mark center of fabric. The red arrow on the chart indicates the center and starting point of your design.

2. Using a 2-length piece of the variegated yarn, at the first float pull the needle and yarn through until half of your yarn is on either side of the float. You will be starting with a double loop stitch that goes above and below the centerline. Stitch from that point to the left (reverse if left-handed), following the chart. Continue stitching until you are about 1½ inches from the edge. Push the needle and yarn to the back and secure the yarn by running under 3–4 floats.

3. Turn the fabric and chart upside down and finish stitching the other half of Row 1.

4. Continue stitching Rows 2–7 as shown on the chart.

5. Note that it is important to then stitch Rows 13–18, using the solid color yarn, before stitching Rows 8–12. It will be very difficult to see where to stitch parts of Rows 13–18 if Rows 8–12 are stitched first.

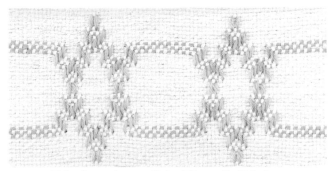

This photo shows stitched Rows 13–18 before Rows 8–12 are stitched as described in step 5.

6. Continue stitching, noting that the final row will be a repeat of Row 1, but you will stitch a loop stitch in place of the double loop stitch where that is indicated on the chart.

7. To finish the bottom half of the afghan, turn both the afghan and the chart and complete this half just as you did the top half.

Finishing

After stitching is complete, see General Instructions for finishing techniques and finish as desired. ●

Surf

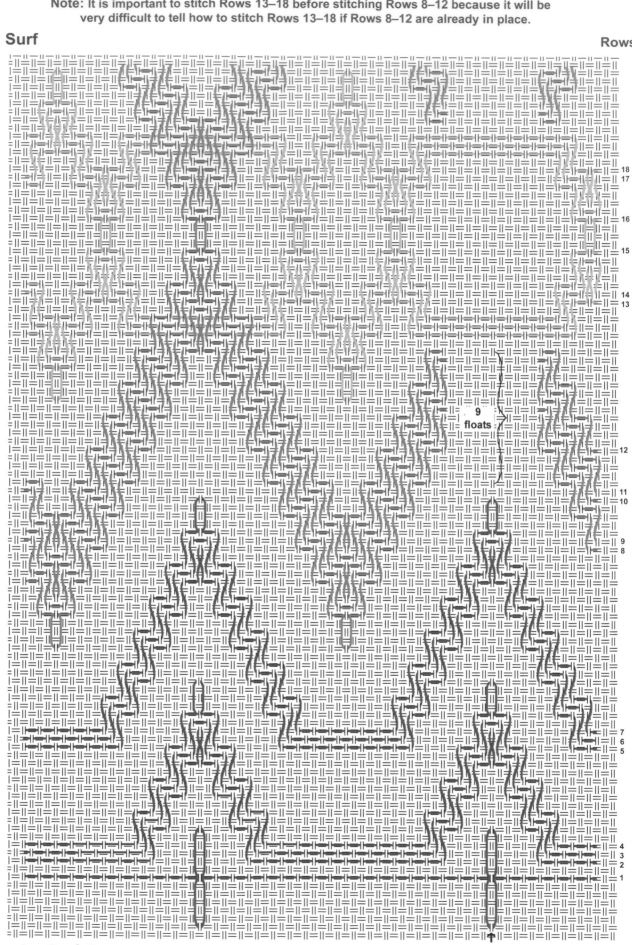

Jasmine

The ever-popular blue and white combination shown in this cozy afghan is timeless and will be the perfect addition to any decor.

Finished Size
44 inches wide x 56 inches long (including fringe)

Skill Level
Intermediate

Materials
- Monk's cloth:
    2½ yds dazzling blue
- Medium (worsted) or fine (sport) weight acrylic yarn:
    500 yds white
- Susan Bates 5-inch steel weaving needle, size 13 tapestry needle or a bodkin
- Basic sewing tools and supplies

Project Note
Refer to General Instructions for fabric preparation, stitch instructions and finishing techniques.

Yarn Lengths
All Rows: 1¾ lengths

Weaving the Design
1. Mark center of fabric. One red arrow on the chart indicates the center of your design. The other red arrow indicates the starting point for stitching and is marked with the words "starting point."

2. Measure down from the center 1¾ inches and mark this spot. This is the starting point for stitching.

3. Using a 1¾-length piece of yarn, at the first float pull the needle and yarn through until half of your yarn is on either side of the float. Stitch from that point to the left (reverse if left-handed), following the chart. Note that after stitching 15 straight stitches, your next stitch will be a slant stitch down as you stitch that section of the design.

4. Continue stitching until you are about 1½ inches from the edge. Push the needle and yarn to the back and secure the yarn by running under 3–4 floats.

5. Turn the fabric and chart upside down and finish stitching the other half of Row 1.

6. Stitch Rows 1–5 as shown on the chart.

7. After stitching Rows 1–5 turn the chart and fabric and do a section of Rows 1–5 going from top to bottom, starting at the green arrow as shown on the chart. These rows will serve as your guide for stitching the rest of the design going from selvage to selvage. Note that when stitching a row from top to bottom, be sure to measure your length of yarn from the top of the fabric to the bottom.

8. Stitch full design from selvage to selvage to desired length.

9. To finish the bottom half of the afghan, turn both the afghan and the chart and complete this half just as you did the top half.

10. After completing all stitching from selvage to selvage, turn fabric and chart and complete all stitching from top to bottom.

Finishing
After stitching is complete, see General Instructions for finishing techniques and finish as desired. ●

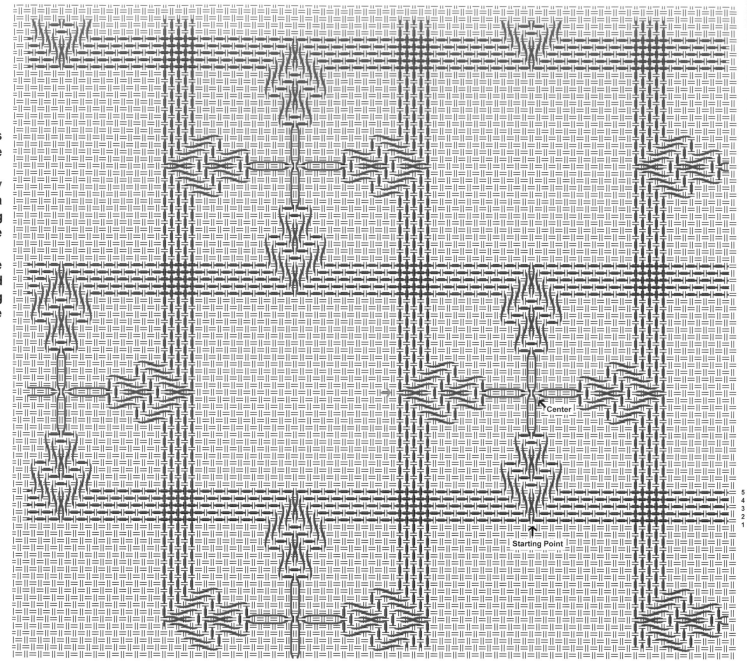

selvage edge

Center

Starting Point

5
4
3
2
1

Notes: On all 4 outside edge sections, there will be no design going to the outside, as shown in this chart section. You will continue with straight stitches until you reach the next design section that goes in (see close-up photo of afghan edge). You may find it useful to use your fabric marking pen to draw a line on the fabric to make sure your sections line up, as indicated by the red lines on the chart.

Jasmine Corner Section

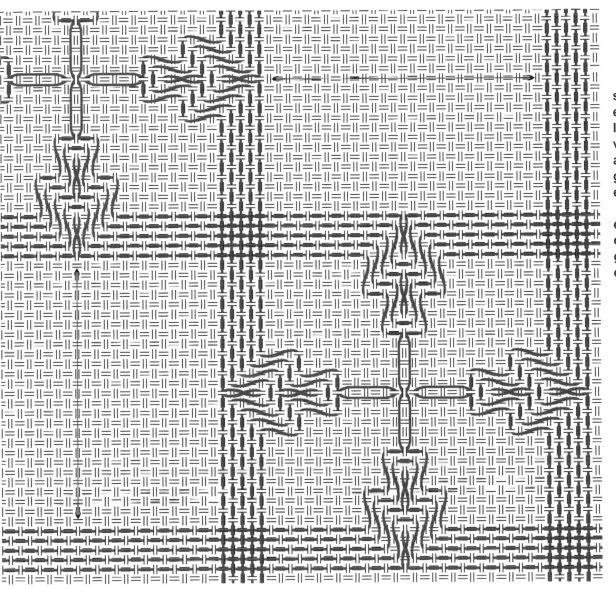

selvage edge

Laurel

The circular stitching of this design gives a floral impression and will look stunning in any chosen color combination.

Finished Size
44 inches wide x 68 inches long (including fringe)

Skill Level
Intermediate

Materials
- Monk's cloth:
  - 2½ yds ice gray
- Medium (worsted) weight acrylic yarn:
  - 300 yds each orchid and raspberry
- Susan Bates 5-inch steel weaving needle, size 13 tapestry needle or a bodkin
- Basic sewing tools and supplies

Project Note
Refer to General Instructions for fabric preparation, stitch instructions and finishing techniques.

Yarn Lengths
All Rows: 2 lengths

Weaving the Design
1. Mark center of fabric. The red arrow on the chart indicates the center and starting point of your design.

2. Using a 2-length piece of the lighter shade of yarn, at the first float to the right of center pull the needle and yarn through until half of your yarn is on either side of the float. Stitch from that point to the left (reverse if left-handed), following the chart. Continue stitching until you are about 1½ inches from the edge. Push the needle and yarn to the back and secure the yarn by running under 3–4 floats.

3. Turn the fabric and chart upside down and finish stitching the other half of Row 1.

4. Stitch Row 2 and then Rows 3–10 as shown on the chart.

5. After stitching Rows 1–10 turn the chart and fabric and do a section of Rows 1–10 going from top to bottom. These rows will serve as your guide for stitching the rest of the design going from selvage to selvage. Note that when stitching a row from top to bottom, be sure to measure your length of yarn from the top of the fabric to the bottom.

6. Stitch full design from selvage to selvage to desired length.

7. To finish the bottom half of the afghan, turn both the afghan and the chart and complete this half just as you did the top half.

8. After completing all stitching from selvage to selvage, turn fabric and chart and complete all stitching from top to bottom.

Finishing
After stitching is complete, see General Instructions for finishing techniques and finish as desired. ●

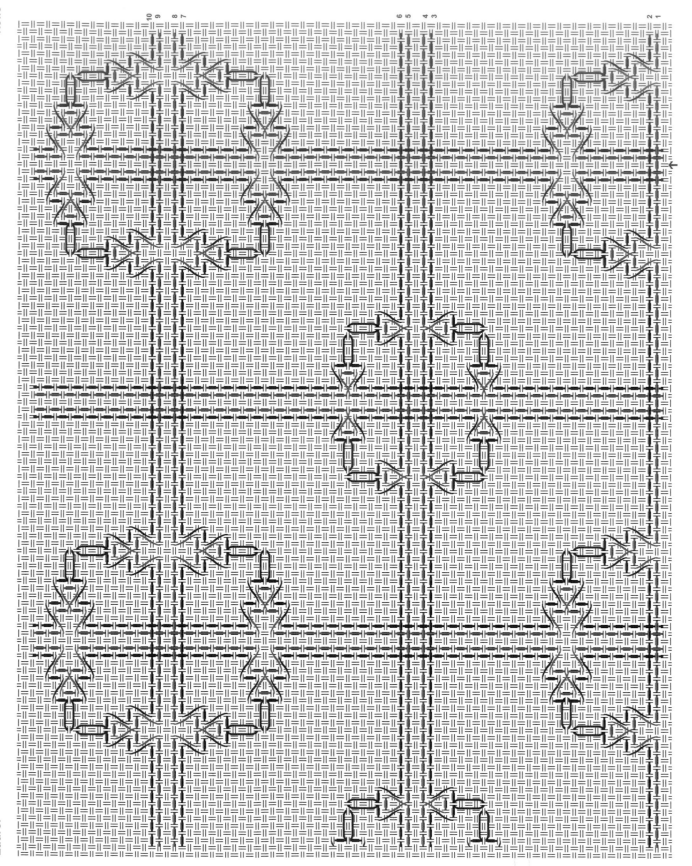

Laurel

Annie's® Published by Annie's, 306 East Parr Road, Berne, IN 46711. Printed in USA. Copyright © 2018, 2021 Annie's. All rights reserved. This publication may not be reproduced in part or in whole without written permission from the publisher.

RETAIL STORES: If you would like to carry this publication or any other Annie's publications, visit AnniesWSL.com.

Every effort has been made to ensure that the instructions in this publication are complete and accurate. We cannot, however, take responsibility for human error, typographical mistakes or variations in individual work. Please visit AnniesCustomerService.com to check for pattern updates.

ISBN: 978-1-59012-920-3

456789